Instant RubyMine Assimilation

Utilize the RubyMine IDE to develop your own
Ruby on Rails applications

Dave Jones

BIRMINGHAM - MUMBAI

Instant RubyMine Assimilation

First published: November 2013

Production Reference: 1221113

Published by Packt Publishing Ltd.
Livery Place
35 Livery Street
Birmingham B3 2PB, UK.

ISBN 978-1-84969-876-4

www.packtpub.com

Credits

Author
Dave Jones

Reviewer
J. Pablo Fernández

Acquisition Editor
Kevin Colaco

Mary Nadar

Commissioning Editor
Sruthi Kutty

Technical Editors
Veena Pagare

Ankita Thakur

Project Coordinator
Amey Sawant

Proofreader
Linda Morris

Production Coordinator
Melwyn D'sa

Cover Work
Melwyn D'sa

About the Author

Dave Jones is a developer and teacher living in Spokane, Washington. He has worked with many of the top Fortune 500 companies during the last 30 years of his career.

Dave has a Bachelor of Science degree in Computer Science from Cal Poly, Pomona and has a Masters of Technology Management degree from Pepperdine University. He has always had a love for computers. He started his career by fixing Apple computers in the early 1980s. He continued on his career path by working at Rockwell Space Division where he had the opportunity to work on various Space Shuttle ground and control systems.

Dave continued his varied career by entering into the burgeoning Internet software industry, where he worked on developing white-label forum/bulletin board systems for many different startup companies. Some of these companies included Apple Computer, Microsoft, WebMD, Cisco, New York Times, UK Guardian, Dr. Phil and Oprah shows, Citicorp, Reader's Digest, Edmunds.com, Sony, Kodak, and many other fortune 500 companies. Throughout this interesting career, he was able to learn many of the technologies that are in use today and decided that he wanted to give back to the software community by teaching some of his life-long skills to new developers beginning their new careers.

Dave began teaching at a Spokane Community college in the Software Development department in 2008. He currently teaches many different technologies including Ruby, Ruby on Rails, PHP, Agile development, CSS/HTML, JavaScript, jQuery, mobile development with Java on the Android OS, as well as Objective-C on Apple iOS devices. He records his lectures and makes them publically available on YouTube where thousands of developers around the world are benefiting from his expertise. He is also the owner of a small software consulting company that helps pay for his teaching hobby.

Dave has a passion for computers, Internet, and building software. He truly enjoys the interaction and satisfaction that comes from the creation of software tools.

I would like to thank Karin, who has been my girlfriend for 34 years and wife for 28 years, for being so supportive during the writing and editing process of this book. I would also like to thank my kids, Becky and Tim, who are a daily inspiration to me.

About the Reviewer

J. Pablo Fernández is a second generation programmer who started coding at the age of seven with a CZ Spectrum (a licensed clone of the ZX Spectrum). His professional career started at age 16 interning for a software security company and a software shop producing telecommunications billing software.

He developed a fair amount of free software and became a member of the KDE project working in its accessibility module. After getting bored with C++, Pablo embarked on a quest to find, or create, the perfect programming language. A quest that obviously took him to Lisp, Smalltalk, Haskell, and eventually he settled with Ruby.

Among his achievements he counts: developing a web app in C, back in the day when that didn't sound as crazy as it is, working for Google, writing a piece of code to route calls in a call center that has been working for years routing millions of calls without a single bug ever found out, crafting open source code that took on a life of its own.

Today, he is the CTO of a startup he co-founded in 2011 called Watu, creating an application for temporary staffing agencies. When he's not drowning in e-mails, he's using RubyMine for his daily job, coding a Ruby on Rails application.

www.PacktPub.com

Support files, eBooks, discount offers and more

You might want to visit www.PacktPub.com for support files and downloads related to your book.

Did you know that Packt offers eBook versions of every book published, with PDF and ePub files available? You can upgrade to the eBook version at www.PacktPub.com and as a print book customer, you are entitled to a discount on the eBook copy. Get in touch with us at service@packtpub.com for more details.

At www.PacktPub.com, you can also read a collection of free technical articles, sign up for a range of free newsletters and receive exclusive discounts and offers on Packt books and eBooks.

http://PacktLib.PacktPub.com

Do you need instant solutions to your IT questions? PacktLib is Packt's online digital book library. Here, you can access, read and search across Packt's entire library of books.

Why Subscribe?

- ▸ Fully searchable across every book published by Packt
- ▸ Copy and paste, print and bookmark content
- ▸ On demand and accessible via web browser

Free Access for Packt account holders

If you have an account with Packt at www.PacktPub.com, you can use this to access PacktLib today and view nine entirely free books. Simply use your login credentials for immediate access.

Table of Contents

Preface

A long time ago, in a country far away, a new technology was created to help the down trodden masses of Ruby on Rails developers. This technology excited those in the collective who sought to assimilate such high technology, as they strove to perfection.

"We too are on a quest to better ourselves, evolving toward a state of perfection."

—From Borg Queen, Star Trek – First Contact.

This technology was developed to help navigate the various aspects of developing Ruby on Rails projects. The requirement for many different files and their management, various windows of logs, consoles, database tables, and tests is a difficult task that RubyMine tries to envelop in an all-encompassing **Integrated Development Environment** (**IDE**). This is a technology that is worthy of assimilating to its fullest extent.

This small book is designed to help readers assimilate the RubyMine technology, as quickly as possible, so that you can get back to developing your own technologies and websites with the Ruby language. It will cover the basics of installation, customization, developing, debugging, and testing code all the way through deployment all within the comforting environment of RubyMine.

The JetBrains developers have spent many years perfecting the RubyMine system and are always on the cusp of new technologies that the Ruby and Rails communities utilize. They incorporate those into the program very quickly and have numerous updates of the software throughout the year. It is software that is written in Java, so it easily runs on almost any platform you can think of including Mac OS X, Windows, and various varieties of Linux.

Take some time to become familiar with the RubyMine IDE and your productivity will increase many times as the tool will begin to get out of your way, so you can code to perfection. You can customize the interface to your liking, even using key commands such as VIM to edit your code if that is your desire.

Have fun learning and assimilating this technology into your own collective.

What this book covers

First contact - installing Ruby and RubyMine (Must know), will show you how to download and install the RubyMine software, making sure that you also have the Ruby language installed as well.

First communication – saying hello (Must know), shows how to set up your environment and projects within RubyMine and how to write your first Ruby program to make sure everything is correct.

Getting comfortable with your new skin (Should know), shows how the various panels and windows work within RubyMine, as well as how to customize the look and feel of the environment.

Managing your implants (Should know), explains the use of Ruby Gems and how to manage those from within the RubyMine environment by using the Prawn Gem and creating a customized PDF document.

Creating your first progeny (Should know), walks you through the creation of a Ruby on Rails project, including the use of the scaffolding and code generation that has made Rails so popular – all from the comfort of the RubyMine project. No need to leave the collective for anything.

Running and debugging your progeny (Should know), will show you how to debug a Rails project along with the various stack, variables, breakpoints and watch windows that make debugging your program a breeze.

Manipulating your tech (Become an expert), explains the use of the built-in Rails Console and **Interactive Ruby (IRB)** that is available directly in the RubyMine environment and how it interacts with the rest of the project.

Testing your tech (Become an expert), explains that testing is a key component in keeping your programs free of bugs and Rails does this very well. This recipe also explains how to write, maintain, and execute the tests inside the RubyMine environment.

Ensuring your legacy (Become an expert), walks you through establishing best practices in using a **Version Control System (VCS)** such as Git and SVN. These tools are essential to ensure that your hard work and code are not lost. RubyMine has excellent support for integrating directly with these and other version control systems.

Refactoring and maintaining your tech (Become an expert), reveals some of the magic that RubyMine offers in terms of maintaining your code base as it grows to expand beyond the collective. It will show tools such as automatic refactoring of code, duplicate code finders and establishing best practices while RubyMine analyzes your code for you.

Strengthening your tech against intrusion (Become an expert), shows how to utilize the SimpleCov Ruby Gem to run reports on how well your testing is covering all of the lines of code in your project.

Monitoring your extremities (Become an expert), explains the use of the ingenious built-in database manipulation tools that are available directly in the RubyMine environment including direct queries, tables, and the creating, reading, updating, and deleting of records in your database without having to go through your interface or launching a console application.

Deploying your progeny to expand your empire (Become an expert), will finally walk you through using the Capistrano Gem, along with the built-in server communication tools of RubyMine (FTP, SFTP, and so on) to upload and maintain your production application for the public to use.

What you need for this book

A preliminary familiarity with Ruby on Rails would be helpful. You will need to have the Ruby language installed on your computer, along with the RubyMine software from `http://www.jetbrains.com/ruby`.

Who this book is for

This book is designed to help the beginners to intermediates Ruby or Ruby on Rails developers, who wish to increase their skill set and improve their effectiveness and efficiency as a developer. The RubyMine IDE software will do just that and this book will guide you along the way.

Conventions

In this book, you will find a number of styles of text that distinguish between different kinds of information. Here are some examples of these styles, and an explanation of their meaning.

Code words in text are shown as follows: "Open the Disk Image (DMG) and drag the RubyMine file from the DMG to your `Applications` folder."

A block of code is set as follows:

```
puts "Hello Biological Life Form. We are the Borg."
puts "We will add your biological and technological distinctiveness to
our own."
puts "Resistance is futile."
```

Any command-line input or output is written as follows:

```
sudo apt-get install subversion
```

New terms and **important words** are shown in bold. Words that you see on the screen, in menus or dialog boxes for example, appear in the text like this: "Select the **Open** button to continue".

Reader feedback

Feedback from our readers is always welcome. Let us know what you think about this book—what you liked or may have disliked. Reader feedback is important for us to develop titles that you really get the most out of.

To send us general feedback, simply send an e-mail to `feedback@packtpub.com`, and mention the book title via the subject of your message.

If there is a book that you need and would like to see us publish, please send us a note in the **SUGGEST A TITLE** form on `www.packtpub.com` or e-mail `suggest@packtpub.com`.

If there is a topic that you have expertise in and you are interested in either writing or contributing to a book, see our author guide on `www.packtpub.com/authors`.

Customer support

Now that you are the proud owner of a Packt book, we have a number of things to help you to get the most from your purchase.

Errata

Although we have taken every care to ensure the accuracy of our content, mistakes do happen. If you find a mistake in one of our books—maybe a mistake in the text or the code—we would be grateful if you would report this to us. By doing so, you can save other readers from frustration and help us improve subsequent versions of this book. If you find any errata, please report them by visiting `http://www.packtpub.com/support`, selecting your book, clicking on the **errata submission form** link, and entering the details of your errata. Once your errata are verified, your submission will be accepted and the errata will be uploaded on our website, or added to any list of existing errata, under the Errata section of that title. Any existing errata can be viewed by selecting your title from `http://www.packtpub.com/support`.

Piracy

Piracy of copyright material on the Internet is an ongoing problem across all media. At Packt, we take the protection of our copyright and licenses very seriously. If you come across any illegal copies of our works, in any form, on the Internet, please provide us with the location address or website name immediately so that we can pursue a remedy.

Please contact us at copyright@packtpub.com with a link to the suspected pirated material.

We appreciate your help in protecting our authors, and our ability to bring you valuable content.

Questions

You can contact us at questions@packtpub.com if you are having a problem with any aspect of the book, and we will do our best to address it.

Instant RubyMine Assimilation

Welcome to *Instant RubyMine Assimilation*. This book will take you through the RubyMine technology and help you become an expert with the use of this amazing programmers' tool for Ruby and Ruby on Rails programs. Resistance is futile—you will be assimilated and will become a happy, proficient, and efficient programmer as a result.

First contact – installing Ruby and RubyMine (Must know)

This recipe will describe the options available for installing RubyMine on the three major platforms—Windows, Mac, and Linux. It will briefly cover the steps for installation of the most recent version.

Getting ready

In order to proceed, you must have already installed a version of the Ruby programming language. The installers for these can be found at `http://www.ruby-lang.org/en/downloads/`.

It is recommended that you download the latest version of Ruby if you are a beginner, which is v2.0. Follow the instructions on the site mentioned previously, depending on your particular operating system.

RubyMine is an application that is written in Java and requires the Java Runtime Environment to work. We will need to download and install the appropriate version of Java as well. If we don't install Java first, then RubyMine will download and install the appropriate version for you the first time it starts. Java installation programs can be found at `http://java.com/en/download/manual.jsp`.

How to do it...

We will now install the actual RubyMine software depending on your operating system.

RubyMine can be found at `http://jetbrains.com/ruby`.

Let's have a look at the steps involved in installing RubyMine on a Mac OS X system:

1. Point your browser to the previous address and download the free trial of the software. This will be in the form of a standard Mac OS X disk image (DMG), as shown in the following screenshot:

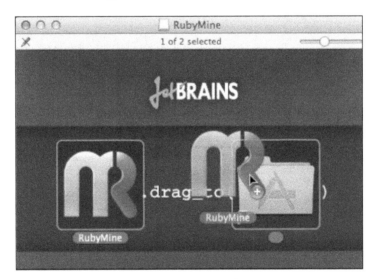

2. Open the Disk Image (DMG) and drag the RubyMine file from the DMG to your `Applications` folder. As shown in the following screenshot, you can now open RubyMine from your `Application` folder by double-clicking on the RubyMine application:

Figure 1.2

3. The first window that you will see is the standard Mac OS X security warning about opening an application from the Internet, depending on your security settings. Select the **Open** button to continue.

4. We will then be presented with the opening Welcome window in RubyMine. We have successfully installed RubyMine and can proceed to the next lesson.

Now, let us look at the steps involved in installing RubyMine on Windows OS:

1. Download the RubyMine installer from `http://jetbrains.com/ruby`.

2. Click on the RubyMine executable and the first window that you will see is the standard Windows security warning about opening an application, depending on your security settings.

3. Select the **Run** button to continue. You will get the following RubyMine setup wizard window:

4. Follow the standard installation steps and select the defaults for the options presented.

5. When the installation finishes, you will be given an option to run RubyMine. Do this and you will see a screen that will ask you to import your settings from a prior version and then a screen asking for your license.

6. If you have a license, enter the two pieces of information into the fields provided and then hit **OK**.

7. Otherwise, just select the option **Evaluate for free for 30 days** and you will have your 30-day trial of the software. You can always enter your license later—after you have been assimilated.

8. Continue on and agree to the license agreement, and you will then be shown a screen similar to *Figure 1.2*, the screen showing the message **Welcome to RubyMine**.

Last but not least, let us look at the installation of RubyMine on a Unix environment.

Most of the X-Windows types of environments in the Unix/Linux world work the same, but we are now going to see the Ubuntu installation:

1. Point your browser to the same URL `http://jetbrains.com/ruby` and select the **Download Free Trial** link. This will begin the download of a `.tar.gz` file and depending on your environment, your browser might ask you to open it with the **Archive Manager** option, as shown in the following screenshot:

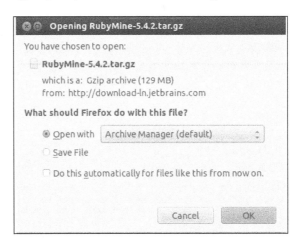

2. Select **OK** and the archive manager will show us a folder of the uncompressed files.

3. Click on the **Extract** button on the top toolbar of the archive manager and select your home folder to save the folder into.

4. Once extracted, we can then navigate to the new RubyMine folder and we will see a file called `Install-Linux.tar.txt`.

5. Follow the instructions contained in this file to complete the installation.

    The main item to pay attention to is the second option in the file:

    2. Open a console (ctrl-alt t) and cd into "{installation home}/bin" and type:

    ./rubymine.sh

    to start the application.

    Doing this will begin the application installation process.

6. A screen showing the options to agree to the license and the option checked for the 30-day trial will be presented with a screen like this:

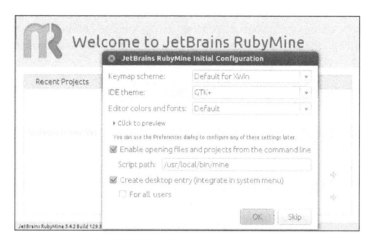

7. Select the defaults for now and hit **OK** to continue.

There's more...

If you run into any errors, some of the solutions are found below. If you have any other problems, you will have to consult the RubyMine website help system.

If you get an error while running the `rubymine.sh` file in Linux (Ubuntu) like the following:

ERROR: Cannot start RubyMine

No JDK found. Please validate either RUBYMINE_JDK, JDK_HOME or JAVA_HOME environment variable points to valid JDK installation.

In this case, you must install a Java Development Environment first and then re-run the `rubymine.sh` file as before.

To install Java on Ubuntu, you must enter several commands. There is a good tutorial on installing the Oracle JDK found at `http://askubuntu.com/questions/55848/how-do-i-install-oracle-java-jdk-7`.

Please note that the OpenJDK is *not* recommended for use with the RubyMine software.

Once this is complete, you can continue with the RubyMine installation as before.

First communication – saying hello (Must know)

Now, we will create a simple application/program along the lines of a Hello World program to make sure the environment is set up correctly, while explaining some of the initial features of the IDE as we go.

Getting ready

You should have already started the assimilation process by completing the recipe *First contact – installing Ruby and RubyMine (Must know)*. If not, go back and restart the assimilation process.

How to do it...

When starting to learn a new language, it is customary to say hello, so let's get started:

1. Open RubyMine and you will be presented with the **Welcome to JetBrains RubyMine** window:

2. Select the option **Create New Project**.

3. Use the name **HelloWorld** in the first box and leave the other two options as default. We are going to start with a simple Ruby application, even though RubyMine can create many different types of project such as a Ruby on Rails project and Twitter Bootstrap Web project.

4. Your next task is to create a new Ruby file that we can use to begin building our first program.

5. Navigate to **File | New ...** and you will be presented with a list of various choices of files to create.

6. Choose the **File** item, which is simply a Ruby file.

7. Name it `helloworld.rb`. Don't forget the `.rb` extension, as this is necessary to distinguish it from a simple text file, which it really is anyway.

8. Now, type in the following program into this new document that you created:

```ruby
puts "Hello Biological Life Form. We are the Borg."
puts "We will add your biological and technological
distinctiveness to our own."
puts "Resistance is futile."
```

This is your first Ruby program in RubyMine! Let's run it using the following steps and see what happens:

1. Navigate to **Run | Run** and you will see a window similar to this:

2. Select the **helloworld** configuration and it will execute your first Ruby script. The output of your program should then be shown in a window panel below your `helloworld.rb` file. Each `puts` command prints out the string to the console and appends a carriage return to the end automatically. RubyMine captures this output in the window at the bottom of the program.

You have successfully begun your assimilation into the collective—there is no stopping you now.

How it works...

RubyMine keeps everything inside its various panels so that you don't have to keep switching between your editor, a terminal/console window, and your browser. It lets you see the output of your programs in the **Run** panel at the bottom of the window, so you can compare the output with what you expected your code to do.

When the main project window opens, you will see a **Tip of the Day** window, similar to the following screenshot:

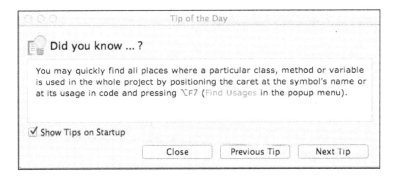

I highly recommend that you maintain this tip window while you are processed through the assimilation stage, as it is much easier to learn a few things a day rather than everything all at once. Your internal Borg buffers will overflow otherwise.

With the Borg it is all about efficiency so that assimilation can happen that much quicker.

There's more...

Each time you create a new project or run a specific file, a new *configuration* is created so that it is easier to switch between running tests, Rails development, or simply a Ruby program file. Once a configuration is created, it is available in a pull-down menu at the top, as shown in the following screenshot:

When you select a particular configuration, you can then just hit the green arrow button to run or the green button with a bug on it to debug the files in that configuration.

If you want to run a different configuration, just select it from the menu and hit the green arrow. This makes it more efficient to switch between different files or environments.

Possible errors during execution

If you get any errors while running, first check to see that you entered *exactly* what is in the preceding program. If you still have errors, it might be your Ruby installation and what RubyMine thinks is your Ruby installation. To check that, select the **Settings** menu item (Mac OS X it is the preferences item in the RubyMine menu, on Windows and Linux it is the **Settings** command from the **File** menu).

This is the main window for setting all of the hundreds of attributes of your RubyMine software.

Select the item **Ruby SDK and Gems** from the left side of this window. You will then be able to select which version of Ruby that you want RubyMine to utilize for your programs.

Once you have selected a version of Ruby, you must then hit the **Apply** button at the bottom of this window on the right. You can also install a new version of Ruby here and install and manage the Gems needed for your various projects. A **Gem** is a standard way of distributing libraries of Ruby code for sharing among developers and projects.

The "Has_Many" options in RubyMine

While you are at the **Settings** window, go ahead and explore around and select the various items on the left to see what options are available to you. You are provided with a large number of ways to customize and change how your new assimilated tool will work for you and the common good of the collective.

Getting comfortable with your new skin (Should know)

We will now investigate how to navigate and customize the RubyMine environment, including windows and panel placement, configuration options, tools, and settings.

Assimilation is easier if you are comfortable with your skin.

RubyMine has a wide variety of options and configuration changes that you can make to precisely match your work style. It allows the use of TextMate plugins and even lets you emulate the VIM text editor if you are so inclined to such madness.

Let's start by changing the basic template that comes with RubyMine into an alternate color structure.

Getting ready

Start RubyMine and open the `HelloWorld` project that we created earlier.

How to do it...

To change the colors and fonts by switching themes, follow the steps listed below:

1. Click on the item ❊ in **Settings** from the **Tools** menu. On the left-hand side of the **Settings** window, there is a setting named **Editor**.

2. Click on the gray arrow to open up this setting, as shown in the following screenshot:

3. Then, click on the **Colors and Fonts** setting. This window will let you change the overall theme for the entire RubyMine window system.

4. Click on the **default** pull-down menu and select the theme **Darcula**.

5. Hit **OK** at the bottom of this window and RubyMine will confirm that you want to change the look and feel of the program.

6. Select **OK** in this dialog box and your theme will be set. RubyMine will then ask you to restart the program and you will then be able to see your changes completely. The environment should now look something like this:

![RubyMine IDE screenshot showing species_controller.rb open with project tree and code editor]

There's more...

All of the settings, colors, fonts, sizes, and so on can be modified through these various settings dialogs and saved as your own custom theme.

We can reset the default colors by selecting the **Appearance** option in the **Settings** window. There is a pull-down menu that has **default** and **Darcula** in it under the heading of **Theme:**. The RubyMine environment is made up of various panels that fit together on the screen. You have full control to modify your workspace for easier assimilation. Each panel can be resized, pinned, docked, floating, and split.

The panels all have a common menu that looks like the following screenshot:

There is a menu item for each of those main controls as follows:

- ▶ **Pinned Mode** – If this option is selected, this means that the panel will remain open even if the focus moves away from the panel

- ▶ **Docked Mode** – If this option is selected, this means that the panel is part of the entire RubyMine window structure

> ▶ **Floating Mode** – If this option is selected, this means that the panel can become its own window completely and moved out of the structure, even into another screen entirely

> ▶ **Split Mode** – If this option is selected, it allows for multiple views to occupy the same panel

In order to maximize the screen for writing code specifically, select all of the panels and uncheck the **Pinned** menu. Now, click on the text window in the center and all of the panels should now be hidden against the main frame of the RubyMine window. There is one more button at the bottom-left corner of the main window that looks like a square. Press that button and even the thick frame will be removed. Now, your screen is ready to construct some serious code.

If you want any of the panels back, you just have to click on the specific panel button on the thick frame to reopen the panel.

Managing your implants (Should know)

Now, we will learn how to utilize RubyMine to manage your Gems and external libraries used for your Ruby on Rails programs.

Getting ready

Start RubyMine and open the `HelloWorld` project that we created earlier. We will be adding an implant to enhance your assimilation process into the collective.

How to do it...

We will now use a Gem in RubyMine by showing the following simple example using the Prawn Gem:

1. Right-click on the `HelloWorld` project folder in the left project panel and add a new file to your project. Name it `pdf.rb`.

2. Add the following code to this new file:

```ruby
require 'prawn'
Prawn::Document.generate("hello.pdf") do |pdf|
  pdf.font "Courier"
  pdf.stroke_color = "ff0000"
```

```
pdf.line_width = 5
pdf.stroke do
  pdf.circle([300, 300], 100);
  pdf.circle([350, 320], 20);
  pdf.circle([260, 325], 20);
  pdf.curve [270, 250], [340, 250], :bounds => [[270, 270],
  [275, 220]]
end
pdf.move_down(300)
pdf.font_size = 36
pdf.fill_color "000000"
pdf.draw_text("You will be assimilated!", :at => [40, 40])

pdf.line_width = 1
pdf.stroke_color = "0000ff"
pdf.move_to([0, 0])
grid = 11
num_lines = 51
size = (num_lines - 1) * grid
pdf.stroke do
  51.times do |idx|
    pdf.line([0, idx*grid], [size, idx*grid])
    pdf.line([idx*grid, 0], [idx*grid, size])
  end
end
end
```

3. Now, right-click on the open source file and select Run pdf. You should get an error similar to **in 'require': cannot load such file -- prawn (LoadError)**. This means that you do not have the required technology to continue the assimilation process. We need to add some Ruby Gems to allow our program to continue.

4. Open the **Settings** panel and select the **Ruby SDK and Gems** panel from the left-hand list. This is where we also changed the version of Ruby that we are using. This panel will allow us to install some specific Ruby Gems that we need.

5. Hit the button **Install Gems...** and you will see a screen like the following:

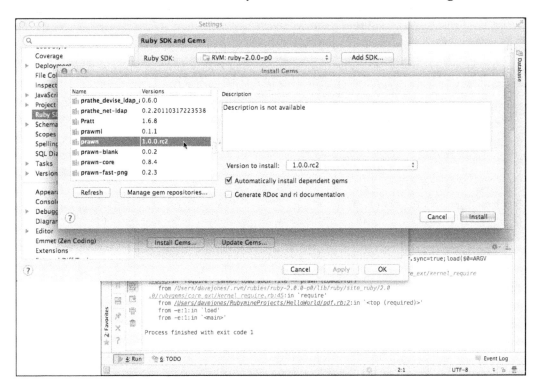

6. Start typing the name of the Gem you wish to install, which in this case is prawn and the search will begin immediately. Scroll to the right Gem.

7. Select the Gem in the list at the left-hand side and then hit the button **Install**. RubyMine will then run the Gem system and install the Gem and all of its appropriate dependencies into your system.

8. When it is complete, select the prawn gem in the list on the right and you will see the description panel filled with various aspects of the gem for your browsing pleasure.

9. Once completed, go back and re-run the pdf.rb program.

10. Since this program actually generates a PDF file, we need to find where it saved the file. In the project window on the left, hit the icon that looks like the following:

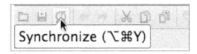

This will synchronize the files inside the folder with the project list. You should now be able to see the file `hello.pdf` in the project window.

11. Double-click on this and you will see this file in whichever application you have on your computer that displays PDF files. You should see something like the following:

How it works

The code that we typed in is a simple use of the Prawn Gem. It first requires the Gem code and then starts a block of code that will begin generating the `hello.pdf` file on the disk. Each command then sets properties of the text, size, colors, circles, and finally draws a grid of lines on the page.

Creating your first progeny (Should know)

Now it is time to create and run a simple Ruby on Rails application using RubyMine exclusively.

Getting ready

Open RubyMine and navigate to **File | New Project**. From this window, you can now select what type of project to begin with. RubyMine gives you several options that you can use later. Right now, select **Rails application**, as shown in the following screenshot:

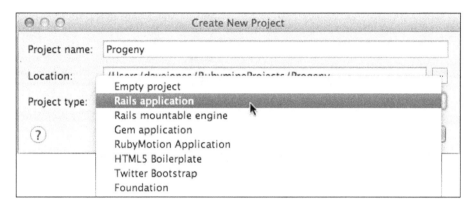

Hit **OK** and you will see the next settings window which allows you to select which version of Rails you would like to use in your project, along with the JavaScript library and database configurations.

Select the checkbox for **Preconfigure for selected database** and choose the **sqlite3** option, as shown in the following screenshot. Leave the rest as default and hit **OK**.

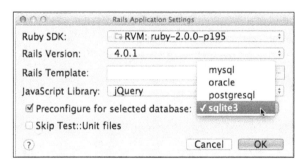

How to do it...

Now that you have created a new Rails project, RubyMine takes over and starts using Rails to generate all of the files and configuration necessary for a complete project, including running the command `bundle install` at the end. This will make sure that you have all the proper Gems installed for your Rails project.

Now, we can run what we have and see that everything is installed correctly, using the following steps:

1. At the top of the window, select the green arrow to run the **Development: Progeny** configuration. Running, in this case, means that it will start the default Rails webserver, Webrick, and begin listening on port 3000 for web browser requests.

2. Once it is running, open your favorite browser and go to the address `http://localhost:3000`, and you should see the opening Rails **Welcome Aboard** screen.

3. Click on the link **About your application's environment**, you can see some details about your installation including the various version numbers of Rails and Ruby, and the database that your application will be using.

Now, we can build some features for our app. Let's begin by creating an interface to our database of species that we have already assimilated. For this, we can use the Rails generators to build the scaffolding of our application that gives us something to build on.

All of the functionalities of Rails can be accessed from within the RubyMine environment, as shown in the following steps, so it is not necessary to go out to a command window at all:

1. To run the generators, we just need to navigate to **Tools | Run Rails Generator**.

2. As you type, the list is filtered to match your selection. Select the **scaffold** generator and hit **Return**:

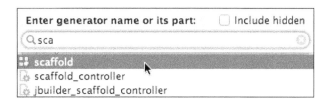

The following window gives us the opportunity to name our table and the various fields that it will contain. The database table will become the name of our model as well.

3. Type the following into the top text box:

```
Species name:string identification:integer assimilated:Boolean
```

4. Leave the other settings at their default and hit **OK,** as shown in the following screenshot:

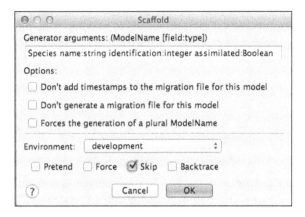

5. Now if you reload your browser window, you should see an error like `ActiveRecord:: PendingMigrationError`.

   Oops! We forgot to do something after creating the code for the database tables. We need to run the migrations that will create the actual tables.

6. Navigate to **Tools | Run Rake Task...** and start typing `db:migrate`. Just like the generator window, the various rake tasks will begin to be filtered by what you type.

7. Hit **Return** and then select the defaults in the next window **Latest migration** and the migrations will be run for you.

8. Now that the tables are created, point your browser to a new location, `http://localhost:3000/species`. You will see the **index** page for your `Species` database table, similar to the following screenshot:

   Click on the links and add some species to your database. The scaffolding that we generated, produced all of the **CRUD (Create Read Update Delete)** forms and screens necessary for managing our `Species` database table, without typing any commands in our terminal or leaving RubyMine at all.

Of course it has no style, but who cares about style? We are the Borg and only care about *technology*!

Ok. Maybe we can spruce it up a little bit. Lets add a Gem called **Bourbon** that helps with the following:

1. Open the Gemfile from the project window and add the following line to it:

   ```
   gem 'bourbon'
   ```

   Now we need to install the Gem by running `bundle install`. We can do this directly from RubyMine by navigating to **Tools | Bundler | Install**.

2. Hit the **Install** button on the window that shows and the Gem will be installed correctly.

3. Now we can edit the CSS file that is in the `App/Assets` folder called `species.css.scss`. Open this file and add the following CSS code to the file:

   ```
   @import "bourbon";
   p {
      @include linear-gradient(to top, white, steelblue);
   }
   ```

4. Reload the page that shows one of the species that you created such as `http://localhost:3000/species/1,` as shown in the following screenshot. Now isn't that much better?

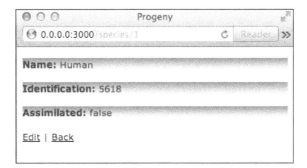

There's more...

Once complete, look at the configuration menu and you will notice that you now have some additional commands in this shortcut menu. RubyMine remembers the tasks and commands that you have executed for you to make it more efficient, as you will likely be running these commands often.

Running and debugging your progeny (Should know)

This recipe covers how to debug your Rails application including watching variables, program stack, and breakpoints.

Although the Borg are perfect, sometimes it is necessary to find problems in our code. To do this, we need to be running the debug version of our code.

Getting ready

Open your `Progeny` project in RubyMine.

How to do it...

Now we get the chance to debug our project, so let's begin. First, select the configuration for development—Progeny just like we were going to run the server:

1. Then hit the green debug (bug) icon 🐞 to the right of the green run arrow.

2. If you have never debugged a Rails application, RubyMine will detect that you are missing some Gems and ask if you want to install what is necessary to continue debugging. Hit the **YES** button and RubyMine will begin installing the gems.

   Your application will now be ready to initiate a debugging session. The server is already running, but we can set a breakpoint anywhere in the Rails program to inspect what is going on at a deep level.

3. In the `Controllers` folder within the `app` folder, open the file `species_controller.rb` and set a breakpoint on the line **27**. This is done by simply clicking on the line right next to the number **7** like this:

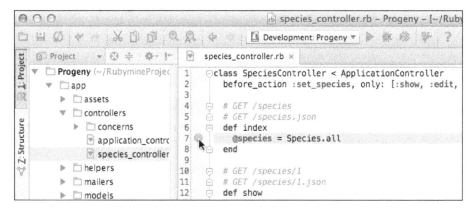

Now we need to get the application to execute this part of the code. Since this is the `Create` method, it means that we must be in the process of creating a new `Species` record in our table.

4. Click on the **New Species** link in the browser or go to the link `http://localhost:3000/species/new`.

   This brings up the form that allows you to enter the values for the table.

5. Enter some values such as `Human` for the name, `5618` for the identification, and check the assimilated checkbox.

6. Select the **Create Species** button, RubyMine will be brought to the front window and you will see a screen that looks like the following:

The bottom of the screen is divided into three panels: The stack **Frames** on the left, the available variables in the middle, and the **Watches** panel on the right.

The **Frames** panel lets you look at the various program threads as well as the stack frames for each thread. This can be very useful to determine the context in which your breakpoint was called.

7. Change the frame and go up to see which method was called before the current method. As you change frames, you will see the variables change along with it, showing you the local variables available in that particular stack frame.

8. Change the frame back to the `create` method so that we can continue.

9. The middle panel is where you can inspect variables as you step through the lines of code.

    Select the little arrow next to the `params` variable in the center panel. It should look similar to the following screenshot:

10. Select the little arrow next to the `species` variable that is inside the `params` variable; you will see the three variables from the HTML form that were sent to the server.

11. Right-click on the `@species` variable and select the **Add to Watches** menu. This variable will now be shown in the **Watches** panel on the right.

    Now move through the code and let's watch this variable change.

    There are five buttons that control the execution of the program in the debugger, as shown in the following screenshot:

    In order from left to right they are: step over, step into, force step into, step out, and run to cursor. The most used is the step over button which we will click now. Once clicked, notice that the `@species` instance variable in the **Watches** window is no longer nil, but has a value.

12. Open the variable in the **Watches** window.

13. Scroll down to find the `@attributes` variable and open that by clicking on the gray arrow. You will see the various properties of the actual `@species` object that contains the same values from the `params` hash that were sent to the form. These were put into place by the `Species.new` code that we just stepped over.

14. Notice that the `created_at` and `modified_at` properties of this variable are still nil. This is because the new object that we created has not yet been saved.

15. Click on the line **30** of the previous source file of the debugger windows which has the code: `if @species.save`.

16. Click on the debug button **Run to Cursor**. The program will continue executing until it gets to this line.

17. Now, press the button to step over and the `@species.save` command will be executed. If the saving operation worked without error, then the program should now be on the line **31**.

18. Look at the `@species` variable in the **Watches** window and you will see that the two date properties will now be filled in with the current date and time.

19. To continue normal operations, you can hit the green arrow on the left-hand side of the debugging windows and the program will continue to execute.

There's more...

There are so many different options that we can control while debugging and too many to cover in this small book. We can even add conditions to our breakpoints. There are some other windows that we can take advantage of while debugging, which are very useful. The right-most button in the debug controls, **Evaluate Expression**, allows us to execute any Ruby expression and inspect variables at the same time.

Add a breakpoint to the line **7** of the `species_controller.rb` file and display the URL, `http://localhost:3000/species`. When the debugger comes to the front, hit the **Evaluate Expression** button. This will bring up a window that lets us add some code. Add the following code to the top input box:

```
Species.find_by_name("Human")
```

Hit the **Evaluate** button at the bottom of the window and you should now see the results in the window, along with arrow navigation to expand and contract the various elements of this variable, as shown in the following screenshot:

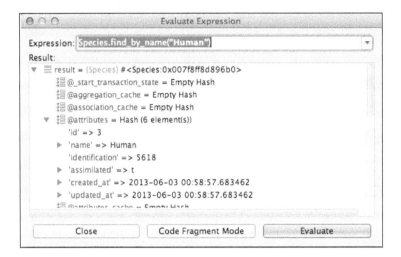

Manipulating your tech (Become an expert)

This recipe will show you how to start the Rails console and inspect your code and database interactively.

Getting ready

Open your `Progeny` Rails project in RubyMine.

How to do it...

RubyMine allows you to run both the **Interactive RuBy** (**IRB**) console as well as the Ruby on Rails console. They both run in an interactive window at the bottom of your editor much like the debugger and output windows. Perform the following steps:

1. On the **Tools** menu, select **Run Rails Console** and RubyMine will ask you which environment you would like to load into the console. This lets you inspect/change your debug, test, or production environments directly. The **default** option gives the development environment.

2. Select **OK** and the console will open.

The Rails console prompt `>>` means that it is ready for input from the keyboard.

Type `2 + 2` and hit **Return**. The result should be `4` as you can see in the following screenshot. This is just like the IRB console, in that you can type Ruby expressions and they will be evaluated interactively.

```
Run ▦ Rails console: Progeny
   Loading development environment (Rails 4.0.0)
   Switch to inspect mode.
   >> 2 + 2
   4

   >> puts "You WILL be assimilated!\n" * 3
   You WILL be assimilated!
   You WILL be assimilated!
   You WILL be assimilated!
   nil


   >>

 ▸ 4: Run    ⬥ 6: TODO   ▦ Version Control   ▦ 9: Changes   ▦ 0: Messages
```

3. Let's perform some database lookups using Rails syntax.

4. The proper syntax for Rails 4.0 is something like the following, which you can type in and see the result:

```
Species.where(assimilated: true).load
```

The result will be something like this:

```
  Species Load (0.2ms)  SELECT "species".* FROM "species" WHERE
"species"."assimilated" = 't'
#<ActiveRecord::Relation [#<Species id: 3, name: "Human",
identification: 5618, assimilated: true, created_at: "2013-06-03
00:58:57", updated_at: "2013-06-03 00:58:57">]>
```

How it works...

We can see that the console returned an array of `Species` objects that matched that query. It even showed us the SQL query that was used to get the data directly from the database.

There are many wonderful tutorials and tricks online that we can make use of to learn more about the console, starting with the official Rails Guides: `http://guides.rubyonrails.org/`.

Testing your tech (Become an expert)

Testing your application is an important and often overlooked aspect of writing good code. This recipe will show how to write some tests for your application using the minitest-reporters Gem and run the tests interactively. This will give you an overview of using tests to make your application much more robust. In addition, we will explore the use of **fixtures** to create some reliable test data as input for your tests.

Getting ready

Open your `Progeny` Rails project in RubyMine.

How to do it...

In order to use the built-in testing tools inside of RubyMine, there is one Gem that we need to install first, which can be done using the following steps:

1. Add the following line to your Gemfile:

    ```
    gem 'minitest-reporters'
    ```

2. Navigate to **Tools** | **Bundler** | **Install** and the Gem will be installed and added to your project.

Now, we need to decide what our test will be, which can be done using the following steps. When we ran the Rails generators to create our first `Species` table in the recipe, *Creating your first progeny (Should know)*, Rails also created some pre-made testing files for us automatically. These are all stored in the folder called `Test`.

1. Expand this folder in the **Project** window and you will find a file called `test_helper.rb`.

2. Open this file and add the following lines to the top of the file:

    ```
    require 'minitest/reporters'
    MiniTest::Reporters.use!
    ```

3. Add the previous lines right below the third line, which should be something like this:

    ```
    require 'rails/test_help'
    ```

4. Save the file and then expand the `Models` folder.

5. Open the file contained inside called `species_test.rb`, which was automatically generated from the scaffold generators for us.

6. Replace the following three commented-out lines:

```
# test "the truth" do
#   assert true
# end
```

Replace the previous code with the following testing code:

```
test 'Full Species Assimilation' do
  @species = species(:not_assimilated)
  assert_equal @species.full_species, "Human 1 has not been
  assimilated.", 'Full Species Not Assimilated incorrect'

  @species = species(:assimilated)
  assert_equal @species.full_species, "Human 1 has been
  assimilated.", 'Full Species Assimilated incorrect'
end
```

One more thing we need that these tests rely on is a file called `fixture`. Fixtures are a way of defining the data that is necessary for a particular database record that can be loaded before each test to populate databases. This is shown in the following steps:

1. Expand the folder inside the `test` folder called `fixtures`.

2. Open the file contained within called `species.yml`.

3. Replace the text in this file with the following code:

```
assimilated:
  name: Human
  identification: 1
  assimilated: true
  notes: Only partially assimilated

not_assimilated:
  name: El-Aurian
  identification: 1
  assimilated: false
  notes: Guinan's Species
```

Now, in order to run the tests, we need to run another rake task specially designed for these types of tests. Perform the following steps to do so:

1. Right-click (*ctrl* + click on Mac) on the word `Species` in the following code line in the `species_test.rb` file in RubyMine.

```
class SpeciesTest < ActiveSupport::TestCase
```

2. This will bring up a menu that will let you run the tests for this module, as shown in the following screenshot:

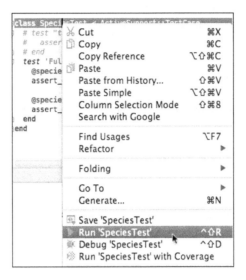

3. If everything has gone correctly, you should see tests running in the bottom panels, as shown in the following screenshot:

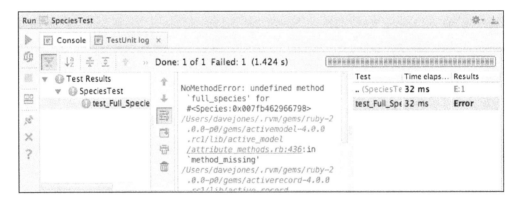

The **undefined method** error is expected since we have not yet written the code for that. Perform the following steps for writing this code:

1. Open the file from the `app` folder, the `models` folder, and the file called `species.rb`. This looks like a good place to add our model-level method called `full_species`. That method is written for you in the following step.

2. Copy and paste the following code into this file, replacing the code that is there:

```
class Species < ActiveRecord::Base
  def full_species
    "#{name} #{identification} has #{(assimilated? ? '' : 'not')}
been assimilated."
  end
end
```

This is a simple method designed to merely combine some of the database fields into a common sentence that might be used in several Rails views across the application.

3. Now that we have a method in place, lets re-run the tests as before. This time we can use the configuration pull-down menu at the top of the IDE and just hit the green arrow next to the menu to re-run the same tests. Unfortunately, we still have an error in our code. You will see a long red bar above the testing windows as well as an error message like the following:

MiniTest::Assertion: Full Species Assimilated incorrect.

--- expected

+++ actual

@@ -1 +1 @@

-"Human 1 has been assimilated."

+"Human 1 has been assimilated."

We can tell by the last two lines that we have an extra space where not might be shown depending on assimilation. Let's fix that now using the following steps:

1. Replace the line in the species.rb model file:

```
"#{name} #{identification} has #{(assimilated? ? '' : 'not')}
been assimilated."
```

with this:

```
"#{name} #{identification} has#{(assimilated? ? ' ' : ' not
')}been assimilated."
```

2. Re-run the tests and we should now see a green bar and all tests passing successfully.

How it works...

These tests are assuming that we have a Species method in Model called full_species. This method was written after the test was written This is called **Test Driven Development** (**TDD**) where the tests are written first and the methods to satisfy the tests come later.

This allows the developer to think about how someone would use a method in the rest of the code, which is basically writing the interface to the method first.

The testing program that we wrote is a simple assertion type test that compares two strings to see if they are equal. We defined the method to return a string, so we hard code a string that we expect and compare it with the returned string from our `full_species` method.

The line in the test `@species = species(:not_assimilated)` reads the `species.yml` file from the `fixtures` folder and creates a temporary species database model with the attributes from the `.yaml` file. This lets us test the various attributes of our model with a standard set of testing data that does not change from test to test.

There's more...

There is a button on the left-hand side of the testing panels called **Toggle Auto-test**. If you select this, then the tests will be executed continuously every few seconds so that you can continue to write tests and methods and check your status constantly.

Ensuring your legacy (Become an expert)

There is nothing worse than losing code that you have spent eons writing. RubyMine has some nice built-in tools to manage your version control systems including Subversion and GIT repositories.

Getting ready

Open your `Progeny` Rails project in RubyMine.

Depending on your OS, download and install Subversion and GIT as follows:

- For the Mac OS, subversion is already installed on the Mac OS X versions.
- Git can be installed by downloading the installer for your version of OS X. The images can be found at `https://code.google.com/p/git-osx-installer/`.
- Follow the instructions for the installer.
- For Windows, Subversion can be downloaded and installed by running the appropriate installer for your system from `http://tortoisesvn.net/downloads.html`.
- Git can be installed through the installer `http://msysgit.github.io/`.

- ▶ Follow the instructions for the installer.
- ▶ For Linux OS, subversion can be installed by opening a terminal window and typing:
  ```
  sudo apt-get install subversion
  ```
- ▶ Git can be installed by typing the following command in a terminal window:
  ```
  sudo apt-get install git
  ```

How to do it...

Now that we have subversion and Git installed, we can tell RubyMine which version control system that we want to use for our project. Let's start with Git:

1. Navigate to **VCS | Enable Version Control System...**

   This will bring up a little window that will let us choose which VCS to use for this particular project. We can have different VCSs for each project that we have in RubyMine, as shown in the following screenshot:

2. Select **OK**. This will initiate the Git system and automatically issue the command `git init` on your project.

3. Expand some folders. You will see that all of the files are now color coded in red. This means that the files are not yet under version control, so we need to add them to our local Git repository. This takes two steps: Adding the files and committing the files.

4. To add the entire project, click on the frame panel button at the bottom of the project called **9: Changes**.

5. Click on the link **Click to Browse** which is next to **Unversioned Files**. A new window will open with a list of files in the project.

6. Select the top-level folder and hit the green **+** button on the left of this window. This will add all of the files and folders to the project under the Git staging system. As shown in the following screenshot, the project window will now show all the files with a green color, which means the files are *added* to the local Git repository, but they have not yet been committed:

Now all we need to do is commit the directory using the following steps:

1. Right-click on the `project` folder in the project list and navigate to **Git | Commit Folder**. This will bring up a window like the following:

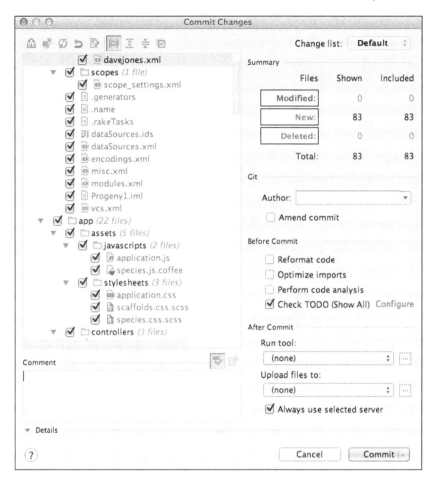

From this window, we can select many options, but the most important is to add a comment in the bottom text box. This comment will follow this commit forever.

2. Type `Initial Project Commit` in this box.

3. Hit the button **Commit** in the bottom-right corner. This will add the files to the Git repository and we can now see that all the files have returned to a black color in the project window. This means that all the files are now under version control. If we make a change to a file, the color will change appropriately. From now on, we can add single files and commit them either individually or as a group, just like the initial commit.

Now let's see how to view changes from different files versus our committed repository changes:

1. Add the following comment line to our `species.rb` file from **app** | **models** above the method that we created earlier:

    `# Return a status string of a particular species`

2. Save the file.

3. Right-click on the opened file and navigate to **Git** | **Compare with Latest Repository Version**. This will show us a window with both versions of the file shown next to each other with insertion and deletions from both versions to show exactly what is different between the two files, as you can see in the following screenshot:

There's more...

The subversion and other version control systems that RubyMine integrates with are basically the same in operation. Explore the subversion system or any other VCS systems that you might be familiar with. Just remember to use one of them to maintain your legacy and not lose your best work.

There are many more controls that you can use with your VCS including comparing full directories, pushing your changes to a remote repository, creating patches, viewing and creating branches, and even integration with GitHub. Feel free to explore all these options on your own.

Refactoring and maintaining your tech (Become an expert)

Once we have written our code, good developers continue to refine that code using techniques called **refactoring**. RubyMine has some excellent tools to help us with that task. In addition, there are database, method, and class viewers and hierarchies. These tools can also help us in locating duplicate code and variables using advanced searching techniques.

Getting ready

Open your `HelloWorld` project that we created earlier in RubyMine.

How to do it...

We will begin with how to refactor some code into a method:

1. Open the `helloworld.rb` file from the project window on the left. We will need to fix a bug in the code first and then we will refactor some of the code into a method that we can reuse later.

2. On the line **24** change the following:

   ```
   51.times do |idx|
   ```

   Change the preceding line to the following:

   ```
   num_lines.times do |idx|
   ```

Now we can select a portion of code that lends itself to being refactored to improve our tech:

1. Select the following entire block of code using your mouse:

   ```
   pdf.stroke do
     num_lines.times do |idx|
       pdf.line([0, idx*grid], [size, idx*grid])
       pdf.line([idx*grid, 0], [idx*grid, size])
     end
   end
   ```

2. Click on the **Refactor This** menu item from **Refactor**. This will bring up a menu like the following:

3. Select **#6 Method...** and a window will be shown that will let us choose the method name and order of parameters that will be passed to the method, as shown in the following screenshot. RubyMine automatically determines which parameters are needed to complete the code.

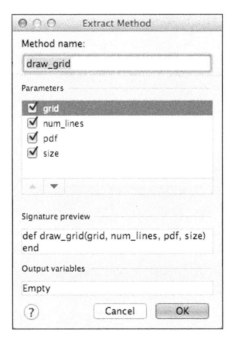

4. Enter the method name `draw_grid`.

5. Hit **OK**.

6. RubyMine will now create a method with the selected code and insert a call to the new method `draw_grid`. The method is placed at the top of the code and should look like the following code:

```
def draw_grid(grid, num_lines, pdf, size)
  pdf.stroke do
    num_lines.times do |idx|
      pdf.line([0, idx*grid], [size, idx*grid])
      pdf.line([idx*grid, 0], [idx*grid, size])
    end
  end
end
```

7. The method call then looks like the following:

```
draw_grid(grid, num_lines, pdf, size)
```

8. Now lets try renaming a variable. Click on one of the variables named `num_lines`.

9. Right-click and navigate to **Refactor | Rename**.

10. Begin typing a new name for this variable, `number_of_lines`.

11. Notice that the variables throughout the file are changed as you type.

If that doesn't get your Borg juices flowing, then you are just not worth assimilating.

There's more...

Another form of refactoring is just the reverse of the *extract method* which is called *inlining*. RubyMine will basically remove the method and put the code back inline with the rest of the code, eliminating a method that might only be used once, for instance.

In addition, RubyMine allows you to create variables from hard-coded values, extract constants, modules, classes—just about anything that you can imagine.

RubyMine can also show us some common errors that can creep into our projects by running an inspection on our codebase and analyzing against some known code style issues. Not all of the issues are errors, but merely coding style items that are brought to our attention.

Select the **Inspect Code** menu item from **Code** and the code will be analyzed and a panel opened similar to the one in the following screenshot. Notice that it finds double-quoted strings where they are not needed and some semicolons at the end of statements that are unnecessary. Ruby has no problem with these issues, but having semicolons are based on some old "tech" that has leaked into our assimilation process that we need to surgically remove. This can be done by simply removing the semicolons and rerunning the code inspection. This is very useful when looking at larger code bases like an entire Rails application.

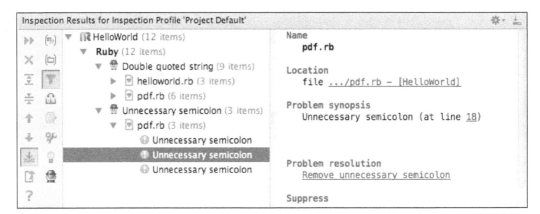

Strengthening your tech against intrusion (Become an expert)

In this recipe, we will begin using the code coverage Gem with the built-in RubyMine tools to enhance your testing regimen and make your code even more robust.

Getting ready

Open your `Progeny` Rails project that we created earlier in RubyMine.

How to do it...

We first need to add the Gem `simplecov` to our Gemfile using the following steps:

1. Open this Gemfile and add the following line:

   ```
   gem 'simplecov', :require => false, :group => :test
   ```

2. Navigate to **Tools | Bunder | Install**.

Now, all we have to do is to run our comprehensive set of tests that we created earlier using the coverage option:

1. Select the **rake test** configuration and then hit the button that looks like **"Run 'test' with Coverage"** .

If you followed the other recipes, then you probably got seven errors in your tests. Oops! Remember that the Borg are only *seeking* perfection, we have not yet arrived! We need to add some text fixtures that we removed earlier using the following steps:

1. Open the `test/fixtures/species.yml` file and add back the following fixtures:

```
one:
  name: MyString
  identification: 1
  assimilated: false

two:
  name: MyString
  identification: 1
  assimilated: false
```

2. Rerun the test with the coverage option and all of our tests should pass. A new panel will open on the right that has the results of our coverage, as shown in the following screenshot:

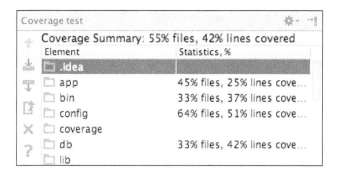

This shows that we don't have many of our lines of code actually tested. Let's generate a report, so we can see more detail:

1. Click on the **Generate Coverage Report** icon which looks like a square with a green arrow point up.

   The next window will ask you where you want to save the file and gives the option of opening the resulting report in your browser.

2. Select this option and hit **Save**.

    Your browser should now open with a report in which you can click on each line and get actual details of which lines of code have not been tested or executed:

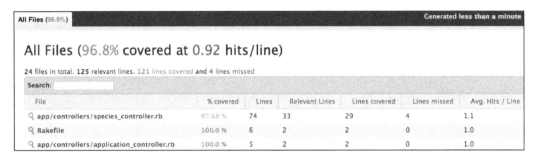

3. Click on the file app/controllers/species_controller.rb.

    You will then get a screen like the following, which shows much more detail about exactly which lines were not tested.

4. The lines in green are tested and they show a little number on the right in a black circle that tells how many times that line of code was executed during the tests. The light red lines show which code has not been executed at all and are ripe for a new test to be written, so we can aspire to 100 percent code coverage:

```
31.    format.html { redirect_to @species, notice: 'Species was successfully created.' }  2
32.    format.json { render action: 'show', status: :created, location: @species }  1
33.  else
34.    format.html { render action: 'new' }
35.    format.json { render json: @species.errors, status: :unprocessable_entity }
36.    end
37.   end
38.  end
39.
40.  # PATCH/PUT /species/1
41.  # PATCH/PUT /species/1.json
42.  def update  1
43.    respond_to do |format|  1
44.      if @species.update(species_params)  1
45.        format.html { redirect_to @species, notice: 'Species was successfully updated.' }  2
46.        format.json { head :no_content }  1
47.      else
48.        format.html { render action: 'edit' }
49.        format.json { render json: @species.errors, status: :unprocessable_entity }
```

5. Now you, the new RubyMine drone, can begin to write the missing tests and continue until you are a perfect 100 percent code coverage expert.

There's more...

If you would like to read more information on SimpleCov, you can find it at `https://github.com/colszowka/simplecov`.

Monitoring your extremities (Become an expert)

RubyMine has more tools that let us manage all aspects of our programming projects. This recipe will concentrate on configuring and using the built-in database tools in RubyMine.

Getting ready

Open your `Progeny` Rails project that we created earlier in RubyMine.

When the project opens, there will likely be a window that comes open like the following:

> **RubyMine Database Integration**
> Rails data sources detected, but some
> additional drivers are required for RubyMine
> to connect to the database
> Download drivers

Click on the link and RubyMine will download and install some Java database drivers so that it can access your Sqlite database (or whichever you are using) from your existing Rails project.

How to do it...

Directly accessing your database fields and structure is much more efficient when we have a nice tool to list and modify our records. RubyMine has the ability to show the tables from your environment directly in the interface, so there is no need to open another tool. Perform the following steps for monitoring your extremities:

1. Click on the **Database** button on the left side of the RubyMine main frame. This will open a panel that looks like the following:

2. Click on the panel and then use the command code as described in the window. (This will be different for each operating system).

3. Select the menu item **Import from sources ...** and then hit **OK** from the next window.

4. Click on the table that shows and open up each level.

5. Double-click on the `id` element of the `Species` table and we will see a window like the following:

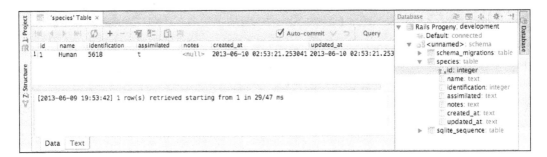

This allows us to view, add, modify, and delete records from our tables easily.

6. Click on the **+** icon, we will then be able to manually add another record to our database.

   If we double-click on one of the cells, we can modify the values that are stored in the database. This is a quick way to edit some mistakes that we made when entering data or to test out a part of our interface. Let's add another record via the table editor.

7. Click on the **+** icon and enter the following information into the cells of the new blank row that is created:

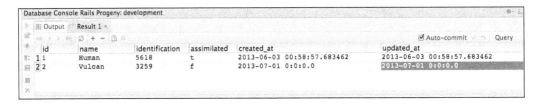

8. Now we have two species in our database. We can edit these items as we please, but please note that updates do not automatically change the `updated_at` field. This is done through the Rails system as it saves a record and we are bypassing that framework completely using this system. We are talking directly to the database.

9. RubyMine also gives us a nice interface to perform direct database queries on our data tables directly.

10. Open the database console by hitting the icon **Database Console** at the top of the **Database** panel. This opens a window in the main editor panel that lets us type SQL queries directly and execute them to get a dataset back, as you can see in the following screenshot:

11. Type the following in the console window:

```
select * from species where assimilated = 'f'
```

12. Select the green arrow button right above the text in the editor panel. Don't select the green arrow which runs a specific configuration.

The results of this direct query will now show at the bottom in a new panel with a database table editor like we had before. It will look something like the following screenshot:

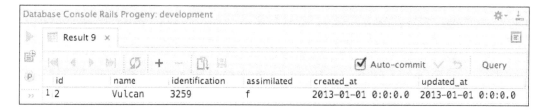

We selected all of the species in our table that have not yet been assimilated. We can now remedy that easily.

13. Double click on the **f** letter in the assimilated column.

14. Change that to t.

See how easy it is to assimilate other species?

Notice that when you changed the field, it disappeared. This is because our query was executed again and found no more species left to assimilate in our database table. Our job is done. We can return to the collective.

Deploying your progeny to expand your empire (Become an expert)

We will now venture into configuring and using the built-in deployment tools in RubyMine. This is the final step in completing your journey through assimilation and ensures the survival of your species. Deployment can be done in many different ways, but we only have time to explore one.

Getting ready

Open your `Progeny` Rails project that we created earlier in RubyMine. Make sure that you have a remote location that will accept a Ruby on Rails project and allows SFTP uploading to this site.

How to do it...

RubyMine can interface directly with a remote server and upload/download files to this site, keeping the files in sync automatically. It also has built-in support for the Capistrano deployment Gem to help with this process of remotely deploying and restarting Rails apps.

It is best practice to use our version control system to deploy our application. It is also easiest if we utilize one of the services out on the Internet to house our repository for us during this process. We will add our existing Git repository that we created in the recipe, *Ensuring your legacy (Become an expert)*, to the GitHub system at `http://github.com` using the following steps:

1. Navigate to **VCS | Import into Version Control | Share Project on GitHub**.

2. This will bring up a window asking for your GitHub account and giving you the opportunity to create one if you don't have one, as you can see in the following screenshot. GitHub is free if you keep your project public and open source, but they also have paid options if that is unappealing to you.

3. After you log in with a valid account, the next window that appears will be for you to name your project and give it a short description. Doing this will create the remote repository on GitHub for us to use later.

4. If we now log in to the GitHub account and navigate to your project, you can copy the Git repository URL, as you can see in the following screenshot, which we can add to our `deploy.rb` file for use in Capistrano:

5. Now, we need to install the Capistrano Gem by adding it to our Gemfile as we have done before, except this time Rails knows that this is a common Gem, so we just need to uncomment out the line in the Gemfile like the following:

```
# Use Capistrano for deployment
  gem 'capistrano', group: :development
```

6. Navigate to **Tools | Bundle | Install**.

7. Now we can use RubyMine tools to start the Capistrano process. We must first navigate to **Tools | Capistrano | Capify Application**.

8. This will create two files: `Capfile` and `config/deploy.rb`.

9. Open the `Capfile` file and uncomment out the following line so that the process will run the precompilation of the assets pipeline after deploying the files to your webserver:

```
load 'deploy/assets'
```

10. Open the `config/deploy.rb` file and edit the following lines using the GitHub repository URL that you copied from your account for the `:repository` line:

```
require 'capistrano-deploy'

set :application, "progeny"
set :repository, "https://github.com/lockersoft/Progeny.git"
set :user, "lockersoft"
```

11. Of course, you would use your own specific information for the server where you are going to deploy your application. There are many different options that you can use from Capistrano to customize your deployment to meet a variety of needs for your particular collective. Too many to show here, so start by looking at the Capistrano Gem documentation found at `https://github.com/capistrano/capistrano`.

12. Once we have our `deploy.rb` file the way we want it, we can commit our changes and *push* those changes to the GitHub remote repository that we created earlier. Navigate to **VCS | Commit Changes**.

13. This will bring up a window that we saw earlier where we can add a message to our commit. At the bottom of the window, instead of selecting **Commit**, we want to select the option **Commit and Push...**:

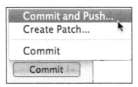

14. This will bring one final window which allows us to choose a different branch. Just hit the **Push** button and our project will be uploaded to the GitHub repository.

15. Now, we are ready to deploy the project. We will let Capistrano do that for us by merely running that script. Navigate to **Tools | Capistrano | Run Capistrano**, which will bring a window to allow us to select one of many tasks to run. The first one we want to run is the `deploy:setup` command. This runs much like the rake tasks and once we select and run a task, it is saved in our task configuration menu at the top of the main project for later use, as shown in the following screenshot:

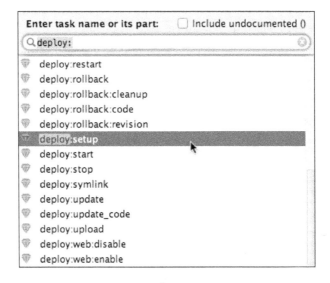

This will create the directory structure that Capistrano needs on your remote server for us.

16. The next Capistrano command is selected from the same menu, but it is simply **deploy**. This will actually issue a command on the remote server to *clone* our Git repository from GitHub into our remote server directory and we will now be ready to access our server.

17. If everything is right in our `deploy.rb` script, which is saying a lot, then the Rails server will be running on our remote server and we can simply connect to the server via a browser like one of our users would.

How it works...

Now, whenever we need to make a change to our application, we just have to follow the following steps in order to deploy those changes:

- ▶ Commit and push our changes to the remote GitHub account
- ▶ Run the Capistrano deploy task
- ▶ Check the server with our browser to make sure everything is working as we expect

We have now successfully deployed our application, which in turn can spawn new drones in our quest for perfection for our entire collective.

There's more...

There are many video tutorials that I have created from my lectures in teaching Ruby, Ruby on Rails, Mobile Development, Java and Android Development, and even PHP development on my YouTube channel. For lectures on all of these, I use the Jetbrains tools such as RubyMine, PHPStorm, and IntelliJ. Check them out at `http://youtube.com/lockersoft`.

In addition, some of the source code examples and code from my other lectures can be found on my GitHub account at `https://github.com/lockersoft`.

About Packt Publishing

Packt, pronounced 'packed', published its first book "*Mastering phpMyAdmin for Effective MySQL Management*" in April 2004 and subsequently continued to specialize in publishing highly focused books on specific technologies and solutions.

Our books and publications share the experiences of your fellow IT professionals in adapting and customizing today's systems, applications, and frameworks. Our solution based books give you the knowledge and power to customize the software and technologies you're using to get the job done. Packt books are more specific and less general than the IT books you have seen in the past. Our unique business model allows us to bring you more focused information, giving you more of what you need to know, and less of what you don't.

Packt is a modern, yet unique publishing company, which focuses on producing quality, cutting-edge books for communities of developers, administrators, and newbies alike. For more information, please visit our website: www.packtpub.com.

Writing for Packt

We welcome all inquiries from people who are interested in authoring. Book proposals should be sent to author@packtpub.com. If your book idea is still at an early stage and you would like to discuss it first before writing a formal book proposal, contact us; one of our commissioning editors will get in touch with you.

We're not just looking for published authors; if you have strong technical skills but no writing experience, our experienced editors can help you develop a writing career, or simply get some additional reward for your expertise.

Ruby and MongoDB Web Development

ISBN: 978-1-84951-502-3   Paperback: 332 pages

Create dynamic web applications by combining the power of Ruby and MongoDB

1. Step-by-step instructions and practical examples to creating web applications with Ruby and MongoDB

2. Learn to design the object model in a NoSQL way

3. Create objects in Ruby and map them to MongoDB

Instant RubyMotion App Development

ISBN: 978-1-84969-652-4   Paperback: 54 pages

A jump start to quickly learn how to program iOS applications with the elegance and simplicity of Ruby

1. Learn something new in an Instant! A short, fast, focused guide delivering immediate results

2. Learn the structure of iPhone and iPad applications

3. Discover how to simplify iOS apps with Ruby

4. Get to grips with how to leverage Ruby libraries to quickly and efficiently write apps!

Please check **www.PacktPub.com** for information on our titles

RubyMotion iOS Development Essentials

ISBN: 978-1-84969-522-0   Paperback: 262 pages

Create apps that utilize iOS device capabilities without learning Objective-C

1. Get your iOS apps ready faster with RubyMotion

2. Use iOS device capabilities such as GPS, camera, multitouch, and many more in your apps

3. Learn how to test your apps and launch them on the AppStore

4. Use Xcode with RubyMotion and extend your RubyMotion apps with Gems

Cloning Internet Applications with Ruby

ISBN: 978-1-849511-06-3   Paperback: 336 pages

Make clones of some of the best applications on the Web using the dynamic and object-oriented features of Ruby

1. Build your own custom social networking, URL shortening, and photo sharing websites using Ruby

2. Deploy and launch your custom high-end web applications

3. Learn what makes popular social networking sites such as Twitter and Facebook tick

Please check **www.PacktPub.com** for information on our titles